Creative with Coluzzle

Wilma Creemers-Joosten

FORTE PUBLISHERS

Contents

© 2002 Forte Uitgevers, Utrecht
© 2002 for the translation by the publisher
Original title: *Creatief met Coluzzle*

Third printing May 2003
ISBN 90 5877 200 4

This is a publication from
Forte Publishers BV
P.O. Box 1394
3500 BJ Utrecht
The Netherlands

For more information about the creative books available from Forte Publishers:
www.hobby-party.com

Publisher: Marianne Perlot
Editor: Hanny Vlaar
Photography and digital image editing: Fotografie Gerhard Witteveen, Apeldoorn, the Netherlands
Cover and inner design: Studio Herman Bade BV, Baarn, the Netherlands

Preface

In Creative with Coluzzle, you make cards using templat0es. Together with Ilonka van Dinteren and Linda, I gave workshops on how to make cards using Coluzzle templates.

I quickly realized that it was great fun and that you could do many different things with the templates. Ilonka helped stimulate me. I enjoyed making this book and hope you also enjoy this Coluzzle technique.

Thanks:

Ilonka for her creative stimulus. Linda and Lidia for their enthusiasm.

Harry and Femke for their help with the computer.

Techniques

Carefully read these instructions and look at the Step-by-step photographs before starting.

1. Templates, a knife and a cutting mat

In order to use the Coluzzle templates, you need a Coluzzle knife and the special, soft cutting mat. The knife pivots and fits exactly in the template's grooves (see photograph 1).

2. The Companion

A Companion is a template which you can use together with another Coluzzle template. There are two Companions: one for the oval and one for the circle. The Companions look the same as the oval or the circle and can be recognized by the C written on the template. The Companion's grooves fit exactly between the grooves of the other two templates. You make narrower strips if you use both templates together. First, place the Coluzzle oval or circle on the paper and cut as many grooves as you wish in the paper. Next, place the Companion on the paper, exactly between the grooves of the other template. Again, cut the desired number of grooves in the paper. You can also miss some grooves to create a wider or narrower strip. There are so many different variations.

3. Using the knife

To make a nice cut, hold the knife upright and place it in the grooves of the template. Allow the knife to follow the grooves of the template. Since the knife pivots, it is easy to cut around the corners.

4. Cutting the template's grooves

The templates have barriers and you usually cut from barrier to barrier. Cut as many template grooves in the paper as you need for your card (see photograph 2).

5. Using small pieces of paper

You can also place the template on a small piece of paper and then cut the grooves. You can then stick this on a card or cut a slit in a card and fold or stick the piece of paper in this slit (see photograph 3).

6. Using the outside of the templates

You can also use the templates to nicely round off the corners of a card. Place the Coluzzle square on the double folded card. Draw around the outside of the template and cut the card out (see photograph 4). To make a rectangular card, first draw around three edges and then place the template against the fold of the card.

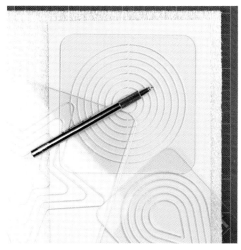

1. Coluzzle templates, a knife and a cutting mat.

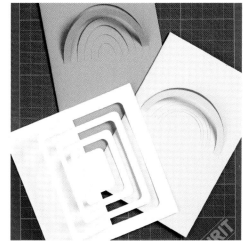

2. Cut the template's grooves.

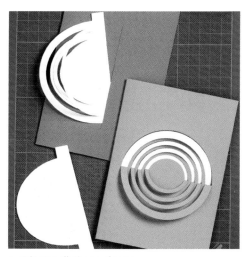

3. Using small pieces of paper.

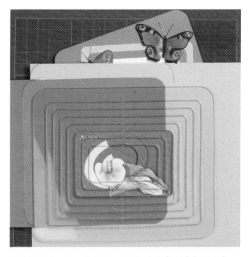

4. Using the template to cut the border of the card.

This will also round off the corners nicely. To make a smaller card, use one of the template's grooves as the edge of the card.

7. 3D cutting

A number of pictures are made into 3D figures. Stick the whole of the first picture on the card. Cut out the picture again, except the background. For the third picture, only cut out what stands in the foreground. Slightly puff up the pictures and stick them on the card using 3D glue.

8. The different types of paper used

Different types of paper are used. These are abbreviated in the text by a letter.
MT = A4 sheets by Canson Mi-Teintes
P = A4 sheets by Papicolor
A = A4 sheets by Artoz

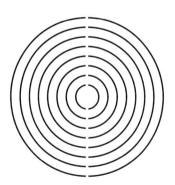

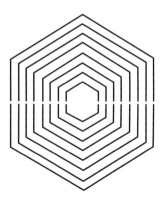

Materials

- Card (Canson Mi-Teintes, Papicolor and Artoz)
- Coluzzle templates: heart, oval, rectangle, circle, hexagon, diamond, star and drop (Kars)
- Companion: circle and oval (Kars)
- Coluzzle cutting knife (Kars)
- Coluzzle cutting mat (Kars)

- 3D cutting sheets
- Vellum parchment
- Star chain stamp (DD045 De Stempelmakers)
- Stamp-pad ink
- Embroidery thread
- 3D scissors
- Photo glue
- Cutting mat
- Hobby knife

- Pencil
- Rubber
- Ruler with a metal cutting edge (Securit)
- Glitter glue (Stickles or Duncan)
- 3D glue
- Gel pens
- Stickers

Cutting pattern card on the cover

Violets

An attractive combination

of colours.

The flowers are finished with transparent glitter glue.

1. A drop with violets
Card: lemon (MT 101) • Vellum parchment • Coluzzle drop • Shake-It cutting sheet (IT329)
Cut an A4 sheet of lemon card through the middle and fold it double. Cut the 1st to 5th grooves of the Coluzzle drop on the left-hand side of the vellum. Cut the 2nd to the 5th grooves on the right-hand side of the vellum. Fold over every other strip. Stick the parchment on the card. Cut out the violets, puff them up and stick them on the card using 3D glue.

2. Circles with flowers
Card: purple (P46) and lilac (MT104) • Shake-It cutting sheet (IT330) • Coluzzle circle and Companion circle
Make a double card (13 x 13 cm) from the purple card. Cut all the grooves of the Coluzzle circle in the card. Place the Companion circle on top and cut the 1st, 4th and 7th grooves in the card. Fold

1.

3.

2.

over every other strip. Cut the same grooves in the lilac card using the Coluzzle circle and the Companion circle. Make a slit in the card. Slide the lilac paper into the slit and stick it in place. Fold over every other strip. Cut out the violets, puff them up and stick them on the card using 3D glue.

3. A hexagon with violets.

Card: purple card (P46) • White vellum parchment • Coluzzle hexagon • Shake-It cutting sheet (IT330)
Make a double card (13 x 13 cm) from the purple card. Cut the 4th to 8th grooves twice in the parchment and fold over every other strip. Cut two slits in the card at an angle and slide the pieces of parchment in these slits. Cut out the violets, puff them up and stick them on the card using 3D glue.

4. Greetings

Card: lemon (MT101), bright yellow (MT400) and apple green (MT475) • Shake-It cutting sheet (IT329) • Coluzzle oval
Cut an A4 sheet of lemon card through the middle and fold it double. Cut the 2nd to 7th grooves of the Coluzzle oval in the card and fold over every other strip. Stick bright yellow and apple green card alternately behind the open strips. Cut out the violets, puff them up and stick them on the card using 3D glue.

Groetjes

4.

Gift labels

You can make these attractive little cards with scrap pieces of card.

Cut the cards as described in point 6 of Techniques and add some transparent glitter glue here and there.

1. Heart with flowers
Card: pale pink (MT193) • Pink vellum parchment • Cutting sheet (3D357) • Coluzzle rectangle and Coluzzle heart
Use the 5th groove of the Coluzzle rectangle to make a pale pink double card.
Cut all of the 6th groove of the Coluzzle heart in the front of the card and cut through the barriers. Stick the heart which you have cut out on the card. Stick the parchment on the inside of the card against the cut out heart.
Cut the picture out and stick it on the card. Cut out the flowers, hearts and feathers again. Puff them up and stick them on the card using 3D glue.

2. White lily
Card: apple green (MT475) and lime (MT100) • Shake-It cutting sheet (IT342) • Coluzzle oval and Coluzzle rectangle
Use the 5th groove of the Coluzzle rectangle to cut an apple green double card. Cut the 6th to 8th grooves in the card and fold a strip over. Cut out the lily and some leaves. Slightly puff them up and stick them on the card using 3D glue.

3. Oval with violets
Card: white, dark pink (MT352) and pale pink (MT103) • Shake-It cutting sheet (IT330) • Coluzzle oval and Coluzzle rectangle • Oval Companion
Make a white double card using the Coluzzle rectangle. Cut the 6th to 8th grooves of the Coluzzle oval in the right-hand side of the card and fold a strip over. Also do this in pale pink card. Slide it between the white card and stick it in place. Cut the 6th to 8th grooves of the Coluzzle oval and the 5th to 7th grooves of the Companion in the left-hand side of the card. Also do this in dark pink card. Slide it in the other card and stick it in place. Fold over every other strip. Cut out the violets, puff them up and stick them on the card using 3D glue.

4. Get well soon

Card: bright yellow (MT400) and warm yellow (MT553) • Shake-It cutting sheet (IT319) • Coluzzle hexagon

Use the 5th groove of the Coluzzle hexagon to make a bright yellow double card. Cut the 7th and 8th grooves in the card and fold the strip over. Stick warm yellow card behind the open strip. Cut out some fruit and stick this on the card.

5. The rings

Card: lemon (MT101) and pale pink (MT103) • White vellum parchment • Cutting sheet (3D357) • Coluzzle circle and Coluzzle rectangle • Circle Companion

Use the Coluzzle rectangle to make a lemon double card according to the instructions given in point 6 of Techniques. Cut the 6th to 8th grooves of the Coluzzle circle in the card. Cut the 6th to 8th grooves of the Companion in the card and fold over every other strip. Do the same for the white parchment and slide it behind the open strips. Stick it in place and slightly fold over the strips. Stick pale pink card on the inside. Cut the picture out and stick it on the card. Cut out the rings again, puff them up slightly and stick them on the card using 3D glue.

6. Oval with fruit

Card: apple green (MT475), lime (MT100) and almond green (MT480) • Shake-It cutting sheet (IT319) • Coluzzle oval and Coluzzle rectangle • Oval Companion

Use the 5th groove of the Coluzzle rectangle to cut an apple green double card. Cut the 6th to 8th grooves of the Coluzzle oval in the card. Do the same in the almond and lime-green cards. Slide both of them behind the open strips and stick them in place. Fold over every other strip. Cut out some fruit, puff it up slightly and stick it on the card using 3D glue.

7. Hexagon with violets

Card: lilac (MT104) and lavender blue (MT150) • Shake-It cutting sheet (IT330) • Coluzzle hexagon

Make a lilac double card using the Coluzzle hexagon. Cut the 6th to 8th grooves in the card and fold over every other strip. Stick lavender blue card behind the strips. Cut out the violets, puff them up and stick them on the card using 3D glue.

Continued on page 32

Fun with flowers

Pretty flowers that do not
need any water.

The pictures are finished with glitter glue.

1. Congratulations
Card: bright yellow (MT400), apple green (MT475) and white (MT335) • Picturel cutting sheet • Coluzzle circle
Make a square card from the bright yellow card as described in point 6 of Techniques. Cut all the grooves of the Coluzzle circle in the card. Rotate the card slightly after every second groove so that the barriers are always in a different location. Fold over every other strip. Cut the 1st, 2nd, 5th and 6th grooves of the circle as far as the barrier in white card, cut the strips out

and stick them on the card. Stick green card (12 x 12 cm) behind the open strips. Make the picture 3D according to the cutting pattern.

2. Get well soon
Card: apple green (MT475), dark green (MT448) and green (MT480) • Picturel cutting sheet • Coluzzle heart
Make a double card (13 x 13 cm) from the apple green card. Cut the top five grooves from the Coluzzle heart in the card and fold over every other strip. Cut the 1st, 2nd, 4th and 5th bottom grooves of the heart in the bottom of the card and remove these strips from the card. Stick green card behind the card at the bottom. Cut the same grooves of the Coluzzle heart out of dark green paper as you have cut in the top of the card. Place these behind the open strips and stick them in place. Slightly fold over the strips.

3. Best wishes

Card: poppy red (MT506) and lilac (MT104) •
Picturel cutting sheet • Coluzzle square
Make a square card from the red card as
described in point 6 of Techniques. Cut the
2nd, 3rd, 4th and 5th grooves of the Coluzzle
square at an angle in the top of the card and
fold over every other strip. Cut half a square
in lilac card using the Coluzzle square's 4th
groove and stick it against the strips. Stick
lilac card behind the open strips. Make the
picture 3D according to the cutting pattern.

4. Congratulations

Card: apple green (MT475), dark green
(MT448) and lime (MT100) • Picturel cutting
sheet • Coluzzle oval
Cut an A4 sheet of apple green card through
the middle and fold it double. Cut a piece of
lime green card which measures 13 x 10.2 cm.
Cut the 2nd to 7th grooves of the Coluzzle oval
in the card and fold over every other strip.
Cut the 3rd to 6th grooves in a piece of apple
green card and fold over every other strip.
Cut the 2nd, 3rd, 5th and 6th grooves in dark
green card and fold over every other strip.

First, stick the dark green card on the card, followed by the apple green card and then the lime
green card. Make the picture 3D according to
the cutting pattern.

5. For no reason

Card: warm yellow (MT553), bright yellow
(MT400) and dark green (MT448) • Picturel
cutting sheet • Coluzzle rectangle
Cut an A4 sheet of warm yellow card through
the middle and fold it double. Cut the 2nd to 7th
grooves of the Coluzzle rectangle in the left-
hand side of the card and cut every other strip
out of the card. Cut the 5th and 6th grooves in
the right-hand side of the card. Cut this strip out
of the card. Stick green and yellow card behind
the strips. Make the picture 3D according to the
cutting pattern.

Marriage

These cards are a pleasure to receive if you are getting married.

Cutting sheet 3D357 is used with these cards. The pictures are finished with transparent glitter glue.

1. Wedding carriage
Card: lemon (MT101) • Silver vellum parchment • Coluzzle rectangle
Make a lemon double card using the Coluzzle rectangle as described in point 6 of Techniques. Cut the 4th, 5th and 7th grooves of the template in the left-hand side of the card and cut out the strips. Cut the 2nd, 3rd, 6th and 7th grooves of the template in the right-hand side of the card and cut out the strips. Stick silver parchment behind the open strips. Cut out the carriage with the horse twice. Carefully cut off all the spokes. Stick the picture on the card using 3D glue.

2. Wreath of flowers
Card: white (MT335) and lemon (MT101) • Yellow vellum parchment • Coluzzle circle
Make a white double card using the Coluzzle circle according to the instructions given in point 6 of Techniques. Cut all the grooves of the Coluzzle circle in the card and fold over every other strip. Cut all the grooves in a piece of lemon card. Place it behind the open strips in the card and stick it in place. Slightly fold over these strips through the open strips. Stick yellow parchment behind the open strips. Stick the picture on the card. Cut out the sprig of flowers, feathers and hearts again. Puff them up and stick them on the card using 3D glue.

3. Swans
Card: pale blue (P42) • Silver vellum parchment • Coluzzle heart
Cut an A4 sheet of pale blue card through the middle and fold it double. Cut the 2nd to 7th grooves of the Coluzzle heart in the card. Do not cut from barrier to barrier, but from the top to the bottom of the heart. Fold the strips over and stick silver parchment behind them. Stick two small bouquets in the top corners. Cut out the swans and stick them on the card. Next, cut out the left-hand swan, all the water lilies and the leaves, as well as the wing of the right-hand swan. Finally, cut out the wing of the left-hand swan and the water lilies again. Puff them up

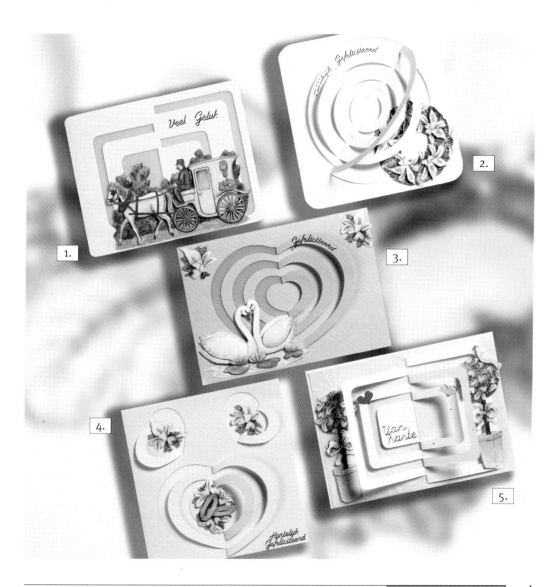

Butterflies

These butterflies are suitable

for any occasion.

The Buttery cutting sheet by Marjoleine is used for these cards. Finish the pictures with a little bit of glitter glue.

1. Butterflies in an oval
Card: lemon (MT101), terra cotta (MT374), salmon (MT384) and corn (MT470) • Coluzzle oval and Companion oval
Cut an A4 sheet of lemon card through the middle and fold it double. Cut the 4th to 8th grooves in the left-hand and right-hand sides of the card. Cut the 3rd and 6th grooves of the Companion in the card and fold over every other strip and weave them together.
Make the same ovals in the terra cotta and salmon card and place these exactly in the open strips.
Stick them in place and fold them over.
Stick corn coloured card (10 x 14.5 cm) to the inside of the card. Cut out the butterflies, puff them up and stick them on the card using 3D glue.

2. Get well soon
Card: lemon (MT101), bright yellow (MT400), crimson (A0549) and mango (A0575) • Coluzzle heart
Cut an A4 sheet of lemon card through the middle and fold it double. Cut the bottom six grooves of the heart in the card and fold over every other strip. Stick crimson, mango and bright yellow card behind the open strips. Cut out the butterflies, puff them up and stick them on the card using 3D glue.

3. For no reason
Card: salmon (MT384), bright yellow (MT400) and ivory (MT111) • Coluzzle square and Coluzzle circle
Make a square card according to the instructions given in point 6 of Techniques. Cut the 2nd to 6th grooves of the Coluzzle square in the card and fold over every other strip. Stick yellow, ivory and then yellow card behind the open strips. Cut out the butterflies, puff them up slightly and stick them on the card using 3D glue.

4. Congratulations
Card: rusty-brown (MT504), bright yellow (MT400) and lily-white (MT110) • Coluzzle square

Cut an A4 sheet of rusty-brown card through the middle and fold it double. Cut the 2nd and 3rd grooves of the Coluzzle square in the card in three different places and fold over every other strip. Stick yellow card behind two open strips and lily-white card behind the other open strip. Cut out the butterflies, puff them up and stick them on the card using 3D glue.

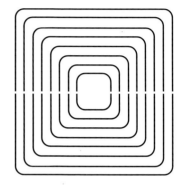

5. Good luck

Card: terra cotta (MT374), rusty-brown (MT504) and salmon (MT384) • Ivory vellum parchment • Coluzzle diamond

Cut an A4 sheet of terra cotta card through the middle and fold it double. Cut six grooves of the Coluzzle diamond in the card and fold over every other strip. Stick rusty-brown and salmon card, as well as ivory parchment, behind the open strips. Cut out the butterflies, puff them up and stick them on the card using 3D glue.

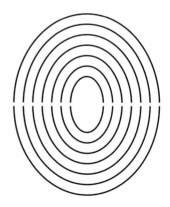

Autumn

These cards are suitable
for wishing somebody
good luck.

*The Autumn cutting sheet by Marjoleine has
been used for these cards.*

1. Hexagons
*Card: rusty-brown (MT504) • Autumn vellum
parchment • Coluzzle hexagon*
Cut an A4 sheet of rusty-brown card lengthways
in two and make a fold on both sides at 3.5 cm
and 7.5 cm. Place the Coluzzle hexagon on the
3.5 cm fold and cut the 5th to 8th grooves in
both sides of the card. Fold over every other
strip. Stick the parchment in the middle. Cut out
the leaves, puff them up and stick them on the
card using 3D glue.

2. Square
*Card: salmon (MT384) and terra cotta (MT374)
• Coluzzle square*
Make a square (13 x 13 cm) from the salmon
card. Cut the 2nd to 7th grooves of the Coluzzle

square in the terra cotta card and fold over
every other strip. Stick this on the salmon card.
Cut out the leaves, puff them up and stick them
on the card using 3D glue.

3. Diamond
*Card: apple green (MT475) • Gold vellum parch-
ment • Coluzzle diamond*
Cut an A4 sheet of apple green card through the
middle and fold it double. Cut the 3rd to 7th
grooves of the Coluzzle diamond in gold parchment. Do not cut from barrier to barrier, but
from a corner to the middle. Fold over every

other strip. Cut a slit in the apple green card. Slide the parchment in this slit and stick it in place. Cut out the leaves, puff them up and stick them on the card using 3D glue.

4. Circles

Card: salmon (MT384) and apple green (MT475)
• Coluzzle circle and Companion circle
Make a double card from salmon card using the Coluzzle circle according to the instructions given in point 6 of Techniques. Cut the 1st to 7th grooves of the Coluzzle circle in the apple green card. Place the Companion on the paper and cut the 2nd, 4th, 6th and 7th grooves in the green paper. Fold over every other strip. Cut a 11.5 cm slit in the paper from the top left-hand corner to the bottom right-hand corner. Slide the green card in the slit and stick it in place. Cut out the leaves, puff them up and stick them on the card using 3D glue.

5. Drop

Card: apple green (MT475), salmon (MT384)
and rusty-brown (MT504) • Coluzzle drop
Cut an A4 sheet of apple green card through the middle and fold it double. Cut the 1st to 5th grooves of the Coluzzle drop in the left-hand side of the rusty-brown card and the 2nd to 5th

grooves in the right-hand side. Fold over every other strip. Cut a strip of salmon card which measures 10 x 14.5 cm and stick it on the card. Stick the rusty-brown card on top of this.
Cut out the leaves, puff them up and stick them on the card using 3D glue.

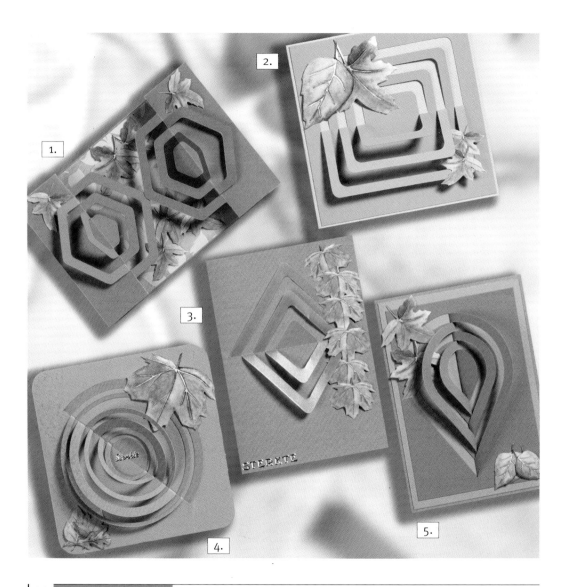

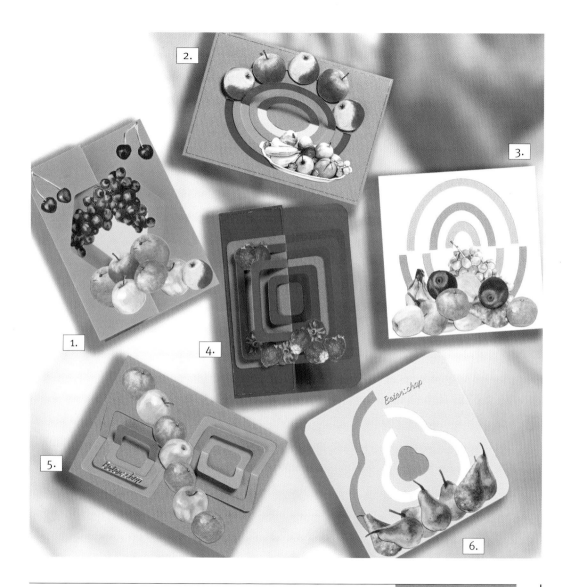

Fruity cards

These cards cheer you

up straight away.

The Shake-It cutting sheet IT319 has been used for these cards.

1. A colourful card
Card: warm yellow (MT553) and bright yellow (MT400) • Coluzzle hexagon
Cut an A4 sheet of warm yellow card through the middle and fold it double. Cut the whole of the 6th groove of the Coluzzle hexagon in the card and half of the 4th groove in the right-hand side of the card. Fold the card in the middle. Cut the 4th groove of the Coluzzle hexagon in both sides of the warm yellow card. Cut through the barriers and stick the hexagon behind the open strip. Cut out the fruit and stick it on the card, slightly on top of each other.

2. A rainbow of apples
Card: apple green (MT475), bright yellow (MT400), warm yellow (MT553) and poppy red (MT506) • Coluzzle oval • Red gel pen
Cut an A4 sheet of apple green card through the middle and fold it double. Draw along a ruler using the gel pen to draw a border around the card. Cut the 2nd to 7th grooves of the Coluzzle oval in the card, not from barrier to barrier, but from the top to the bottom of the right-hand side of the template. Cut through the barriers and fold over every other strip. Stick bright yellow, warm yellow and poppy red card behind the open strips. Cut out the fruit bowl and apples and stick them on the card.

3. A bit of everything
Card: lime (MT100), apple green (MT475) and almond green (MT480) • Coluzzle oval
Make a double card (13 x 13 cm) from the lime green card. Cut the 2nd, 3rd, 5th, 6th, 7th and 8th grooves of the Coluzzle oval in the top of the card. Cut out every other strip. Cut the 1st, 2nd, 4th and 5th grooves of the Coluzzle oval in the bottom of the card and cut out these strips. Stick apple green and almond green card alternately behind the open strips. Cut out the fruit and stick this on the card in various places. The fruit at the front is stuck on the card using 3D glue.

4. Strawberries
Card: poppy red (MT506) and apple green (MT475) • Coluzzle square • Green gel pen

Cut an A4 sheet of red card through the middle and fold it double. Cut the 2nd to 7th grooves of the Coluzzle square in the card and fold over every other strip and cut away the paper at the top left-hand side of the card until the 2nd groove. The bottom card is rounded off using the Coluzzle template. On the right-hand side of the card, stick apple green card behind the 5th and 6th grooves. Also do this on the left-hand side from the 2nd groove. Use a ruler to draw a line on the left-hand side of the card using a gel pen. Cut out the strawberries and stick them on the card.

5. A caterpillar made from fruit
Card: apple green (MT475) and warm yellow (MT553) • Coluzzle diamond
Cut an A4 sheet of apple green card through the middle and fold it double. Cut the 4th to 7th grooves of the Coluzzle diamond in the top right-hand and bottom left-hand corners of the card. Fold over every other strip. Stick warm yellow card behind the open strips. Cut out the oranges and apples and use them to make a caterpillar.

6. Pears
Card: bright yellow (MT400), lime (MT100) and apple green (MT475) • Coluzzle circle and Coluzzle heart

Make a bright yellow double card using the Coluzzle circle according to the instructions given in point 6 of Techniques. Cut the 1st, 2nd, 5th, 6th and 7th grooves of the top of the Coluzzle heart in the left-hand side of the card. Cut the top of the 3rd, 4th and 7th grooves in the right-hand side of the card. Cut all the strips out of the card. Cut out some pears and stick them on the card overlapping each other using 3D glue

slightly and stick them on the card using 3D glue.

4. Wedding rings
Card: pale pink (MT103) • Pink parchment • Coluzzle heart
Make a double card (12.5 x 12.5 cm) from the pale pink card. Cut the middle two grooves of the Coluzzle heart in the top left-hand and top right-hand corners of the card. Do not cut from barrier to barrier, but from the top to the bottom of the heart. Fold the strips over. Cut the 3rd to 6th grooves in the bottom of the card and fold over every other strip. Stick pink parchment behind the open strips. Stick two sprigs of flowers in the small hearts and the rings in the large heart. Cut out the rings again, puff them up slightly and stick them on the card using 3D glue.

5. Congratulations
Card: lilac (MT104) and white (MT335) • Spring vellum parchment • Coluzzle rectangle
Cut an A4 sheet of lilac card through the middle and fold it double. Cut the 2nd to 7th grooves of the Coluzzle rectangle in white paper. Cut a slit in the lilac card. Slide the white card in the slit. Stick it in place and fold over every other strip. Stick the parchment on the left-hand side of the card. Cut out the trees and stick them on the card. Cut out the front of the pot, a part of the bow and the tree tops again. You can also cut out the dove again. Slightly puff up the pictures and stick them on the card using 3D glue.

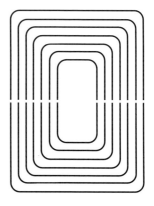

Merry Christmas

Attractive cards for

the festive period.

Use glitter glue to make the pictures sparkle.

1. Lanterns
Card: blue (MT590) • Shake-It cutting sheet (IT339) • Coluzzle hexagon • Star sticker sheet
Cut an A4 sheet of blue card through the middle and fold it double. Fold the card over 5.5 cm from both sides to make a harmonica card. Cut the 2nd groove of the Coluzzle hexagon in the card at the top of the middle section. Repeat this 0.5 cm higher up and cut off the strip. Cut the 2nd groove in the bottom of the card. Repeat this at a distance of 0.5 cm, 1 cm and 0.5 cm from each preceding groove and fold the strips forwards. Cut out the lanterns and the mistletoe and stick them on the card. Stick stars in various places on the card.

2. Oval and Christmas decorations
Card: lavender blue (MT150), lilac (MT104) • Shake-It cutting sheet (IT326) • Coluzzle oval • Companion oval
Make a lavender blue card (15 x 10.5 cm) and fold it double. Cut the 5th to 8th grooves of the Coluzzle oval in the top and bottom of the card. Cut the 4th to 7th grooves of the Companion in the top and bottom of the card. Cut and fold over every other ring and weave them together. Cut the same grooves in the lilac paper. Slide it in the strips at the top of the card and stick it in place. Cut a piece of lavender blue card to a size of 9 x 10 cm and stick it on the bottom of the card. Cut out the Christmas decorations and stick them on the card.

3. Globe with Christmas decorations
Card: blue (MT590) and lavender blue (MT150) • Shake-It cutting sheet (IT340) • Coluzzle circle • Companion circle
Cut an A4 sheet of blue card through the middle and fold it double. Cut a slit along the line of the fold. Cut the 3rd to 7th grooves of the Coluzzle circle in the lavender blue card. Cut the 3rd to 8th grooves of the Companion in the card. Slide this through the slit in the card and fold over every other strip to create a globe. Cut out the Christmas decorations. Thread embroidery thread through the holes, slightly puff up the decorations and stick them on the card using 3D glue. Stick the thread to the strips of the circle using double-sided adhesive tape.

4. Star with an angel

Card: Wine red (A519) • Silver and gold vellum parchment • Shake-It cutting sheet (IT315) • Coluzzle star and Coluzzle circle • Star chain stamp • Gold stamp-pad ink

Make a wine red double card using the outer edge of the Coluzzle circle according to the instructions given in point 6 of Techniques. Cut the 2nd and 3rd grooves of the Coluzzle star in the card. Do not cut from barrier to barrier, but stop at the curve of two points. Fold the strip over. Cut the middle star out of the card and stick gold parchment behind it. Stamp the star chain a couple of times on silver parchment and stick it behind the open strip. Cut out the pictures, puff them up slightly and stick them on the card using 3D glue.

5. Circles with Christmas decorations

Card: lavender blue (MT150) • White vellum parchment • Shake-It cutting sheet (IT340) • Coluzzle circle • Star chain stamp • White stamp-pad ink

Cut an A4 sheet of lavender blue card through the middle and fold it double. Cut the 4th and 5th grooves of the Coluzzle circle in the top and bottom of the card. Cut the 5th and 6th grooves slightly further along the card. Cut the 7th

groove out of the card. Also cut the strips off of the card. Use white stamp-pad ink to stamp the star chain on the parchment a number of times and stick it behind the open strips. Cut out some Christmas decorations. Thread embroidery thread through the holes, puff them up slightly and stick them on the card using 3D glue. Stick the thread at the back of the card using adhesive tape.

Cards on the cover, page 1 and page 3

Poppy (card on the cover)
Card: bright yellow (MT400) and poppy red (MT 506) • Picturel wildflower cutting sheet • Coluzzle circle • Companion circle

Make a bright yellow card which measures 28 x 10.5 cm. Fold this card over at 10 cm and 21 cm to make a harmonica card. Cut a piece of red card to a size of 10 x 9.5 cm and stick it in the middle of the card. Cut the 3rd to 8th grooves of the Coluzzle circle in the yellow card. Place the Companion on this and cut the 2nd to 8th grooves in the card. Fold over every other strip. Take a piece of red paper and make the same circles as in the yellow card. Cut a slit in the left-hand side of the yellow card. Slide the red strip through it and stick it in place. Fold over every other strip and weave them together with the yellow strips. Make the picture 3D according to the cutting pattern (see page 7). Finish the pictures using glitter glue.

Violets (page 1)
Card: lilac (P14) • Spring vellum parchment • Shake-It cutting sheet (IT330) • Coluzzle diamond

Cut an A4 sheet of card through the middle. Fold both sides of the card 4.5 cm and 8 cm from the edge. Cut the parchment to the correct size and stick it on the card. Cut the middle four grooves of the Coluzzle diamond in the card and fold over every other strip. Cut out the violets, puff them up and stick them on the card using 3D glue. Finish the violets using some glitter glue.

Vase of flowers (page 3)
Card: apple green (MT475) and lime (MT100) • Picturel wildflower cutting sheet • Coluzzle circle

Cut an A4 sheet of card through the middle and fold it double. Cut the middle four grooves of the Coluzzle circle in the lime green card. Do this four times. Fold over every other strip. Cut a slit in the card. Slide the strips in the slit and stick them in place.

3D cutting: cut out the entire picture and stick it on the card. For the second layer, do not cut out the bowl of fruit. For the third layer, cut out the flowers and fruit again. Slightly puff up the pictures and stick them on the card using 3D glue. Finish the pictures with some glitter glue.

(continued from page 11)

8. Pink lily

Card: dark pink (MT352), pale pink (MT103) and white (MT335) • Shake-It cutting sheet (IT341) • Coluzzle square and Coluzzle circle • Circle Companion

Make a dark pink double card using the 5th groove of the Coluzzle square. Cut the 6th to 8th grooves of the Coluzzle circle and then the 5th to 8th grooves of the Companion in the card. Fold over every other strip.

Cut the same in the pale pink card. Slide this behind the open strips and stick it in place. Slightly fold over the strips. Stick white card behind the open strips. Cut out the lily and the leaves. Puff them up and stick them on the card using 3D glue.

9. Vase with feathers and hearts

Card: white (MT335) • Silver vellum parchment • Cutting sheet (3D357) • Coluzzle rectangle and Coluzzle oval

Use the 5th groove of the Coluzzle rectangle to make a white double card. Cut the 6th to 8th grooves of the Coluzzle oval in the top of the card and fold the strip over. Cut the 7th groove in the bottom of the card. Stick silver parchment behind the open strips. Cut the picture out and stick it on the card. Cut out the flowers with the leaves, feathers and hearts again. Puff them up and stick them on the card using 3D glue.

10. Circle with violets

Card: white (MT335) and lavender blue (MT150) • Shake-It cutting sheet (IT330) • Coluzzle square and Coluzzle circle • Companion circle

Make a white double card using the Coluzzle square. Cut the 6th to 8th grooves of the Coluzzle circle in the card followed by the 6th to 8th grooves of the Companion. Fold over every other strip. Stick lavender blue card behind the open strips. Cut out the violets, puff them up and stick them on the card using 3D glue.

Thanks to:
Kars & Co B.V. in Ochten, the Netherlands and Ilonka van Dinteren for providing the materials.

The materials used can be ordered by shopkeepers from:
Kars & Co B.V. in Ochten, the Netherlands.